CHÈRE

CHÈRE MAÎTRE

The Correspondence of
Gustave Flaubert and George Sand

Adapted by Peter Eyre

from the translations of
Francis Steegmuller and Barbara Bray

OBERON BOOKS
LONDON

First published in this adaptation in 2002 by Oberon Books Ltd.
(incorporating Absolute Classics)
521 Caledonian Road, London N7 9RH
Tel: 020 7607 3637 / Fax: 020 7607 3629
e-mail: oberon.books@btinternet.com

Chère Maître is based on the correspondence of Gustave
Flaubert and George Sand, published by The Harvill Press as
Flaubert–Sand: The Correspondence, 1993.

A catalogue record for this book is available from the British Library.

ISBN: 1 84002 305 8

Cover photograph: Tom Lucy

Printed in Great Britain by Antony Rowe Ltd, Chippenham.

Contents

Preface

Sometime in the early nineties, Susan Fleetwood, incandescent actress and dear friend, suggested we should work on a recital together. I told her I hated those poetry readings where two actors coyly sing-song their way through their favourite party pieces, and would try to think of something else. Only recently I had read the new Steegmuller/Bray translations of the Flaubert–Sand correspondence, and thought that it might have dramatic possibilities. Fleetwood, who was dyslexic, didn't think she could get through the four hundred or so pages, but did read a review of the book from the *New Yorker*. She responded enthusiastically to the idea and so I started the initially labourious task of making a stage adaptation. After many false starts and interruptions I produced a very long first draft. Fleetwood and I began to read it together one summer, sitting under a tree in my garden. It was thrilling to work with her but also unsettling, because just as Flaubert in the correspondence knows Sand's health is failing but never gets a direct answer when he asks her, 'What is it? Is it serious?', so I knew Fleetwood was fighting illness but she firmly refused to talk to me about it. 'Tra la la – it's nothing', Sand replies to Flaubert, and I would try not to look at her.

Meanwhile I had shown my script to Irene Worth on one of her visits to London from New York where she lived. She had recently performed an acclaimed solo show about Edith Wharton, and I was delighted when she expressed interest in my piece. I thought perhaps she might do it in New York with an American actor. A couple of years later I was on Broadway playing Polonius in *Hamlet*, and one day Irene Worth suggested that if my days were free perhaps we could work on the text together. Inspired by her musical ear and infallible instinct I began to cut, reshape and refine the speeches. Eventually we had a workable text, which we performed for the first time in Sharon, Connecticut at a benefit. I wrote to Fleetwood, whose illness had now forced her to stop working, to tell her of the birth of *Chère Maître*. She wrote me a typically generous letter. Since Irene Worth was perhaps her very favourite actress, she was touchingly pleased that our project was now in safe hands. Six weeks later Fleetwood died.

Irene Worth and I performed the piece over a period of five years in New York, London, and at the Melbourne Festival. Later the BBC broadcast it as a Friday Play under the title of *Dear Master*. There were plans to revive it in New York under yet another title (*Gustave and George* was considered a possibility) but recently Irene Worth died very suddenly.

Saddened as I am by her death, I am comforted by remembering how much she loved the letters of George Sand, especially one of the later ones where she writes to Flaubert: 'Before long you will gradually be entering upon the happiest part of life: old age. It's then that art reveals itself in all its sweetness; in our youth it manifests itself in anguish.' Worth told me often that it was exactly how she felt.

I feel very privileged to have worked on this extraordinary correspondence – which is a dialogue about the nature of art and friendship – with two great artists, two great friends. I would like to dedicate *Chère Maître* to them.

Peter Eyre
London, 2002

Introduction

The publication of Gustave Flaubert's novel *Salammbô* in 1863 was greeted with less than enthusiastic criticisms. George Sand, however, read and so greatly admired it that she wrote a spirited defence of the work which appeared in *La Presse*. Flaubert was more than pleased that the 'Mother of French Literature' had dignified his book with praise. Although he had only met her briefly (and did not admire her writing – he described her literature as the sort in which 'everything oozes, and ideas trickle between words as though between slack thighs'), he sent her an appreciative note and a request for her portrait. Flaubert, the complex literary genius, was flattered by the attentions of Sand, who was a star, and whose exotic and romantic past was the stuff of legends. Sand replied with enthusiasm. Although seventeen years older than Flaubert, she could not resist the exciting possibility of this new friendship. After her first visit to his house at Croisset, where he lived with his mother, she confided to her diary, 'I am mad about him'. Flaubert knew that she was too old for their affection to evolve into a love affair, but he responded eagerly to her tenderness and her motherly concern for his well-being. Anyway Sand, now a wise and kindly grandmother, was quite a different person from the young lover of Chopin and de Musset. So began a deep friendship and one of the greatest epistolary masterpieces of modern times. Their actual meetings were rare. They visited each other in the country a couple of times, and dined together infrequently in Paris. It was in letter writing that their friendship blossomed. Even during the horrific years of the Franco-Prussian War and the Commune, they kept in more or less constant touch. Towards the end of Sand's life in 1876, her profound affection for him as a friend and her respect for his art gave her the courage to write to him a pertinent critique of what she felt were his failings as a writer. He accepted it with good grace, and later, realizing how ill she was, wrote to tell her how much he had enjoyed reading her latest publication. Perhaps there was a hint of hypocrisy in his praise, but he had grown to honour her friendship as a rare gift. He loved her. At her funeral he stood by her grave and wept.

Peter Eyre

Author's note

The term 'Chère Maître' means 'Dear Master'. Flaubert coined this salutation in a letter of 1866, using the feminine form of the adjective with a masculine noun as a homage to his friend, and proving that, at least in this case, the French master of style and verbal correctness would make a concession for the sake of affection.

Characters

GEORGE SAND

GUSTAVE FLAUBERT

Chère Maître was first performed at the Sharon Stage, Sharon, Connecticut, on 29 July 1995, with the following cast:

GEORGE SAND, Irene Worth
GUSTAVE FLAUBERT, Peter Eyre

On one side of the stage, a chaise longue, cushions, a small table – the world of GEORGE SAND.

On the other, a single chair and table – the world of GUSTAVE FLAUBERT.

SAND

Please – you mustn't thank me – I was merely doing what I felt I had to do.

FLAUBERT

I was touched by your goodness of heart: your sympathy made me proud, that's all.

SAND

All I'd heard about *Salammbô* before I read *Salammbô* itself, was unfair or inadequate, and I'd have thought it either cowardly or lazy to be silent. When the critics do their duty I'll keep quiet. You know I'd rather create than judge. I don't mind adding your enemies to my own. A few more one way or the other…

We don't know each other very well but do come and see me when you have the time. It's not far, and I'm always here. I'm an old woman – don't wait until I'm in my second childhood.

Solve a puzzle for me. In September someone sent me an interesting pressed plant in an envelope with no name on the back. It now strikes me the address is in your handwriting. But how could that be? How could you have known that I take a keen interest in botany?

FLAUBERT

Your letter, which I have just received, adds to your article and goes beyond it, and I don't know what to tell you other than, quite frankly, I love you for it. No, it wasn't I who sent you a flower in an envelope last September. But what is strange is that at that same time, in the same fashion, I was sent a leaf.

As for your cordial invitation, I answer neither yes nor no, like a true Norman.

Perhaps I'll surprise you some day this coming summer. Because I greatly long to see you and talk to you.

P.S. I should very much like to have a portrait of you to hang on the wall of my study in the country, where I often spend long months quite alone. Is the request indiscreet? If not, I send you my thanks in advance.

SAND

There aren't many proper portraits of me. When I go to Paris I'll choose something presentable and send it to you. Thank you for the welcome you mean to extend to my face, which is insignificant as you well know.

FLAUBERT

Nothing about you is insignificant, whatever you may say. I'll be delighted to receive your portrait, and shall be proud of it always. I kiss both your hands.

SAND

My friend, this is to tell you I'd like to dedicate my forthcoming novel to you. I want to know if you'll allow me just to put 'To my friend Gustave Flaubert' at the top of my first page.

FLAUBERT

Why, with pleasure of course! With gratitude and affection, dear master. I read Monsieur Sylvestre without once putting it down – and have embellished it with some marginal notes.

SAND

Bring your copy of the book. Write in all the criticisms. Balzac and I used to do this! It doesn't mean you change one another – on the contrary, it usually makes one cling more firmly to one's own point of view. That's why friendship is a good thing even in literature. The first and foremost condition is to be oneself.

FLAUBERT

Dear master, I learn from some worthy people here that the novel dedicated to me has begun to appear. I thank you again, very sincerely and deeply. I'll wait to read it until it's all in print. A book should be gobbled down whole, then re-read – when it is by you.

SAND

I'm going to see Alexandre Dumas at Saint-Valery, and on Tuesday I'll come and see you. Let me know how to get there. I think I'll be well enough, though I have an awful cold. If it gets too much worse I'll send you a wire. But I hope to be able to come; I feel better already.

FLAUBERT

As soon as you reach Saint-Valery, reserve your place in the old rattletrap to Motteville. Otherwise you'll risk being delayed. You'll reach Rouen at one o'clock. There you'll find me at the door of your compartment.

You won't have to attend to anything. So you'll be staying with us.

Music. Pause.

SAND

Great man as you are, you are a good kind boy, and I love you with all my heart. Your own house and garden, your citadel – they're like a dream, and I feel as if I were still there.

Paris seemed quite small yesterday as we came in over the bridges. I feel like going away again. I haven't seen enough of you – of you and your setting.

But I must rush after the children, who are calling for me and showing their teeth.

FLAUBERT

How sweet, how nice it is, your letter which came this morning. For me it is like a continuation of the final, farewell look you gave me the day before yesterday, from the train. We have done nothing but talk about you since you left. Where are you? I am alone, my fire is burning, the incessant rain is falling in sheets, I'm hard at work, and thinking of you.

SAND

And so, my dear Benedictine, you are all alone in your delightful monastery, working and never going out? You're a very special and mysterious being, and yet as meek as a lamb. Every so often I longed to ask you some questions, but I was held back by my great respect for you: my own disasters are the only ones I can handle. Sainte-Beuve, although he's fond of you, says you're terribly dissolute. But perhaps he sees things

through somewhat sullied eyes, like the learned
botanist who says drop-wort is a 'dirty' yellow. This
observation was so wrong I couldn't help writing in the
margin, 'No, it's you who've got dirty eyes.' An artist is
an explorer who oughtn't to shrink from anything: it
doesn't matter whether he goes to the left or the right.
It's up to him, after a bit of experience, to know what
best suits the health of his soul. I think your soul is in a
state of grace because you enjoy working and being
alone despite the rain.

FLAUBERT

I, a 'mysterious being!' Come now! I find myself
revoltingly banal, and am thoroughly bored by the
bourgeois I have under my skin. Sainte-Beuve, between
you and me, doesn't know me at all, whatever he may
say. I even swear to you (by your granddaughter's
smile) that I know few men less 'dissolute' than I. I
have *dreamed* much, but *done* very little. If you want my
confession, I'll make you a full one. A sense of the
grotesque has kept me from slipping into a disorderly
life. I think cynicism is next to chastity. We'll have
much to say to one another about this, if you're willing,
the next time we meet. I hope nothing will prevent
your coming back here with me, not for a day, as you
say, but for at least a week. You will have your room,
'with a table and everything needed for writing.' Is it
agreed? There will be just the three of us, including my
mother.

SAND

I'll come and stay with you for a week – but only on
condition that you don't turn out of your own room. I
can't bear to be a nuisance, and I don't need all that to-
do in order to sleep. I can sleep anywhere – in the

cinders or under a kitchen settle, like a watchdog. Everything's spotless in your house, so it's comfortable anywhere. If the weather's fine I'll make you rush around. If it goes on raining we'll toast our shanks and tell one another our love problems. And the great river will run black or grey under the window. I dream so much and live so little that I'm sometimes only three years old. But the next day I'm three hundred. Isn't it the same with you? Doesn't it occasionally seem to you as if you're starting out on life without even knowing what it is, while at other times you feel weighed down by thousands of centuries of which you have only a dim, painful memory? Where do we come from, and where are we going?

FLAUBERT

I never experience a sense of life that is just beginning. It seems to me, on the contrary, that I have always existed! And I actually have memories that go back to the Pharaohs. I see myself at different moments of history, in various guises and occupations. I was boatman on the Nile, a procurer in Rome, then Greek rhetorician in Subarra, where I was devoured by bedbugs. I died during the Crusades from eating too many grapes on the beach in Syria. I was pirate and monk, mountebank and coachman – perhaps Emperor of the East, who knows?

SAND

You're lucky to have such clear recollections of other lives. A good deal of Imagination and Learning – that's what your 'memory' is! I think *I* was once a plant or a stone. I'm not always sure I completely exist at all, and at other times I feel such an accumulation of weariness it's as if I'd existed too long. Here I am all alone in my cottage.

The gardener and his family live in the lodge, and we're the last house at the lower end of the village, completely surrounded by country – a lovely oasis. Meadows, woods, apple trees just as in Normandy; no big river with its steam hooters and infernal clanking, just a brook flowing silently under the willows; and such silence… Oh, I feel as if I were in the middle of a virgin forest: no voice but that of the little spring forever catching diamonds in the light of the moon. The flies drowsing in the corners of the room wake up in heat from the fire. They went there to die, but when they get near the lamp they go wild with joy, they buzz and dart about and laugh – they even have vague thoughts of love, but it's time to die, and bang! Down they crash right in the midst of the dance. It's all over – farewell to the ball!

FLAUBERT

You're lonely and sad down there: it's the same with me here. Where do they come from, these waves of black depression that engulf one from time to time? It's like a rising tide. You feel you're drowning; you have to escape. At such moments I lie flat on my back. I do nothing – and the flood recedes. You don't know what it is to spend an entire day with one's head in one's hands, in search of a word. With you, the flow of ideas is broad, like a river. With me it's a tiny trickle. I can achieve a cascade only by the most enormous effort. I know them well, the Pangs of Style! I spend my life racking my brain and my heart.

SAND

On the whole I think the joys and sorrows of those of us who work with our brains are too intense.

Why don't you try some time to write a novel with an
artist for a hero, and you'll see what a delicate and
restrained, though strong, current of sap will flow
through him.

An artist is such a fine subject I've never really dared
attempt it. It's too high for a mere woman to aim at.
But it might well tempt you some day. Where's the
model? I don't know. I've never really known any artist
who didn't have some spot on his sun, some aspect of
the grocer. It may be you haven't any such spot; you
should paint your own portrait. I have flaws. I have a
touch of the teacher. I like sewing and wiping babies'
bottoms: I have a touch of the servant. I'm absent-
minded and have a touch of the fool. I wouldn't like
perfection.

Be less cruel to yourself and forge ahead. What you do
seems so easy and prolific, a perpetual brimming over.
I simply can't understand your anguish.

FLAUBERT

I'm not a bit surprised that you fail to understand my
spells of literary anguish. I don't understand them
myself. They exist, however, and are violent. At such
times I no longer know how to go about writing, and
after infinite fumbling I succeed in expressing only a
hundredth part of my ideas. Nothing spontaneous
about your friend! Far from it! These last two days, for
example, I've been casting and recasting a paragraph,
and still haven't solved it. At times I want to weep.
I must seem pitiable to you. How much more so to
myself! My view – contrary to your own – is that
nothing good can be done with the character of the
'ideal Artist.' Art isn't intended to depict exceptional

beings. I feel an unconquerable aversion to putting anything of my heart on paper. I even think that a novelist hasn't the right to express his opinion on anything whatsoever. Has God ever expressed his opinion? There are so many things that I long to spit out, and which I choke down instead.

Any Tom, Dick or Harry is more interesting than Monsieur G. Flaubert, because they are more *general* and consequently more typical. There are days, nevertheless, when I feel I'm moronic. I now have a bowl of goldfish. And they entertain me, they keep me company while I eat my dinner. Imagine taking an interest in anything so inane!

SAND

Not put any of one's heart into what one writes? I don't, I simply do not understand. For my part, I don't see how one can put anything else. Can one separate one's mind from one's heart? What did you mean?

FLAUBERT

I expressed myself badly when I told you 'one shouldn't write with one's heart.' This is what I meant: I believe great art is scientific and impersonal. What you must do is transport yourself into your characters, not turn them into yourself. So: make sure you have a great deal of talent – and, if you can – genius.

SAND

Your old troubadour is beastly unwell today, but that won't stop me from going to Magny's this evening and dining with all our old friends. Well, I know I couldn't kick the bucket in better company. I'd just as soon die by a ditch, if it's the spring.

All I'm fit for today is to write my own epitaph! *Et in Arcadia ego*, of course.

Music. Pause.

FLAUBERT

Well, dear master? What does this mean? Has a letter from you gone astray? I've had no news of you for a long time. I miss you, and worry about you. A kiss while awaiting a few lines in your dear hand.

SAND

It's stupid to be laid up, to lose all notion of oneself for three days, and then to get up as weak as if you'd been doing something useful. However, it was nothing, really, just a temporary inability to digest anything, due to cold, or weakness, or work – I don't know. I haven't done any work for more than a fortnight. I've completely lost interest in anything but my own little ideal of country life, and affectionate friendship.

I don't think I have very long to live, even though I'm better and feeling quite well. I see a sign of this in the great calm, that's beginning to enter my once turbulent soul – 'ever more calm' –

So how is the novel coming along? Your courage hasn't failed? Your solitude isn't getting you down? I imagine it isn't quite absolute, and that there's a lovely lady friend somewhere who comes and goes or lives nearabouts.

FLAUBERT

No, you are not near your end. So much the worse for you, perhaps? But you will live to be old, very old –

like the giants, since you belong to that race. Only, you *must* rest. It astonishes me that you haven't died twenty times, you've thought so much, written so much, suffered so much. Why don't you go to the Mediterranean for a bit, as you'd like to? Blue skies relax and restore one. Life isn't easy! What a complicated business, and so expensive! As for me, I continue to fiddle with my novel. It proceeds at its usual slow pace. Every day I chip away at my coconut, like a convict breaking stones. I'm one myself. Not a convict. A nut. And whatever you may suppose, no 'lovely lady' comes to see me. Lovely ladies have greatly occupied my mind – but consumed little of my time. Whole weeks go by without my exchanging a word with a soul. And at the end of the week it's impossible for me to recall a single day, or any fact whatever. I see my mother and my niece on Sundays, and that's all. My only company is a tribe of rats that make an infernal racket in the garret overhead: I hear them whenever the river stops roaring and there's a drop of the wind. The nights are black as ink. One's sensibility becomes very exalted in such an atmosphere. My heart beats wildly for no reason at all – understandable, in an old hysteric like me. For I maintain that there are male hysterics as well as female, and I am one of them.

SAND

I'd find the kind of solitude you live in delightful when the weather was fine. But in winter it strikes me as stoical! And I have to remind myself that you have no moral need of regular exercise. Now that's all very fine, but it mustn't go on forever. If the novel is going to take longer you must interrupt it or intersperse it with periods of recreation. That's the truth, my friend. Give a thought to the life of the body.

FLAUBERT

I have followed your advice. I have taken some exercise! On Sunday night at eleven o'clock, the moonlight on the river and the snow was such that I was seized by the itch of locomotion. And I walked for two and a half hours – working myself into a state and pretending that I was in Russia or Norway. When the tide came in and cracked the surface of the stream it was superb. I thought of you and wished you were there. For you I have a particular feeling, one I cannot define.

You know, you've never told me what your illness is. What is it? Is it serious?

SAND

Pooh! To hell with it! Tralala! I'm not ill now, only half. The local air is curing me – either that, or patience; or 'the other' me who wants to go on working and creating. What is the illness I'm suffering from? Nothing. Everything's in good condition, but there's something called anaemia, which has been threatening for some years and manifested itself openly in Palaiseau. But everything's improving now, and since yesterday I've even been able to work.
And you, dear friend – you go walking in the snow at night. Rather farfetched for someone who ventures out so rarely; it could easily make you ill, too. It was the sun I prescribed for you, not the moon: we're not owls!

We've just had three spring days. But I bet you haven't been up to your dear orchard that's so pretty and that

I'm so fond of. You ought to climb up through it at noon every fine day, if only in memory of me. The work would flow more freely afterwards.

Have you got money worries, then? I haven't known what they are, since I stopped having possessions. I live off my day's work, like the proletariat; when I stop being able to do a day's work I'll be looking for the next world and shan't need anything more. But you must go on living, and working if you are to live from your pen. Ah, I'm not the person to teach you how to look after yourself.

Oh, how I'd love to go away, to leave at once for sunny climes! But I have neither the money nor the time.

FLAUBERT

No, I do not have what are called money worries. My income is very limited, but secure. Barring the unexpected, I'll be able to keep myself in food and firewood to the end of my days. My heirs are, or will be, rich. (I'm the poor man of the family.) But enough of that. As for earning money by my pen, it's something I've never thought about. One leads a modest country life on what one has. But there are so many other people, more deserving than I, who haven't a sou, that it would be wrong to complain. Besides, railing against Providence is such a common way of going on that one should refrain, if only for good form.

One more word about money, which will be a secret between us. As soon as I'm in Paris I'll be able easily, with no strain whatever, to lend you a thousand francs in case you need it to go to Cannes. No fuss about it, please. Among conventional folk this would be thought improper, I know, but between troubadours much can be dispensed with.

SAND

We really must love one another in earnest, dear comrade, for we both thought of the same thing at the same time. You, who are as penniless as I am, offer me a thousand francs to go to Cannes; and when *you* wrote that *you* were bothered about money, *I* opened the letter I'd written you to offer you the same amount. And then I didn't dare. It was very silly, and you were better than I and actually did it. So my best love for your kind offer, though I don't accept it.

My health has worsened again in the last few days. I don't mind admitting it to you – I haven't the energy to *want* to live. It would be so pleasant just to go off like this, still loving, still loved, at war with no one, not displeased with oneself, dreaming of such marvels in other worlds. When shall we meet? Around December 15th we're christening our two little girls here. You must come. Maurice wants you to, and he'll be very upset if you don't. You can bring your novel and read it to me when we have a break; it will do you good to read it to a good listener. It gives one a chance to tighten things up and get a clearer view of what one's written. Say yes to your old troubadour and he'll be mightily pleased with you. Six kisses if you say yes.

FLAUBERT

You can't imagine the anguish you cause me. Despite my longing to come, I say 'No.' However, I'm torn by the longing to say 'Yes.' It makes me appear to give myself airs – as if I were 'Not to be disturbed'; and that's absurd. But I know myself: if I were to come to stay with you at Nohant I'd spend the next month day-dreaming about the visit. My poor brain would be filled with real pictures instead of the ones I'm at such pains to invent; and my house of cards would crumble to dust.

I'll come to you when I'm 'in a more tranquil state of mind'. Please give Maurice not my apologies but my sad regrets.

Did I tell you that I had a visit from Turgenev? How you would love him!

SAND

Turgenev was more fortunate than we, as he managed to tear you away from your inkpot.

You create an exceptional life for yourself. I also, because of the bohemianism I was born with. I suspect you get more enjoyment from your work than from anything else in the world. It's quite possible that *art* is your only passion, and that your seclusion, over which I fret like the fool that I am, is your form of ecstasy.

FLAUBERT

I am not 'working myself to death', for I've never been better. It's pleasure and torture combined. Nothing that I write is what I want to write. For one doesn't choose one's subjects: they impose themselves. Shall I ever find mine? Shall I ever be able to write a book into which I put my entire self?

As to the secluded life to which I condemn myself being a 'form of ecstasy' – no! But what to do! To get drunk on ink is better than to get drunk on brandy. The Muse, crabbed though she may be, is the source of less grief than Woman! I cannot accommodate the two. There has to be a choice. Mine was made long ago. There remains the question of the senses. Mine have always been my servants. Even in the days of my greenest youth I did with them exactly as I pleased. I am now almost fifty, and their ardour is the least of my worries.

This regime is not very amusing, I agree. There are moments of emptiness, of hideous boredom. But these decrease as one grows older. To be truthful, *living* strikes me as a business I wasn't cut out for! And yet!...

I have nothing, absolutely nothing, to tell you, except that I miss a certain person called George Sand, and that I long for news of said individual.

SAND

A certain person called G. Sand is well, enjoying the weather, picking flowers, observing unexpected botanical eccentricities, making dresses and coats for her daughter-in-law and costumes for puppets, cutting out stage sets, dressing dolls and reading music – but best of all, spending hours with little Aurore.

I am alone at Nohant, as you are at Croisset. Maurice and Lina have gone to Milan to see her father, who's dangerously ill. They left me in charge of the children. I'm with them nearly all the time, and the only chance I get to work is when they're asleep, but I'm lucky to have that to take my mind off things. Aurore is an amazing child. She usually sits on her father's or mother's lap basking in adoration, and cries every day when I'm not there, but hasn't once asked where her parents are. She plays and laughs, then stops and stares out of her beautiful wide eyes and says 'Papa?' – or sometimes 'Maman?' I distract her, she forgets, and then it happens again. Children are very mysterious! I think children's sensitivity should be allowed to slumber as long as possible, and that Aurore would never cry for me if no one ever mentioned me. What do you think?

FLAUBERT

I ought to have been hardened by being brought up in a hospital and playing as a small child in a dissecting room. And yet no one is more easily moved than I by the sight of physical suffering. It's true that I'm the son of a man who was extremely humane, and sensitive in the good sense of the word. The sight of a dog in pain brought tears to his eyes. Yet this didn't impair his efficiency as a surgeon. He even invented some operations that were quite dreadful. I don't agree it's a good thing to expose children to the good, gentle side of life until reason can help them either accept or challenge the bad aspect, for then something terrible is bound to take place in their hearts, an infinite disillusionment. Everything has to be learned, from Talking to Dying. The child and the barbarian do not distinguish reality from fantasy. I remember very clearly that when I was five or six I wanted to 'send my heart' to a little girl I was in love with. (I mean my physical heart.) I pictured it lying on a bed of straw in a basket – the sort of hamper they put oysters in. Our good Turgenev should be in Paris by the end of March. It would be nice if the three of us could dine together. I'm in the middle of paying bills. It makes me irritable, 'naturally'!

SAND

If you need any of the ready, I've got a bit on hand at the moment.

FLAUBERT

Thank you for the offer! At present I'm not in need. Here is the title I've decided on, in desperation:

L'Education Sentimentale
– Histoire d'un Jeune Homme.

So far it best conveys what I've had in mind. This difficulty in finding a good title makes me wonder whether the *idea* of my book, the concept behind it, is absolutely clear.

SAND

I made a point of re-reading your book, as did my daughter-in-law, and some of my young men, all sensitive readers. And we all agree it's as forceful as the best of Balzac's novels and more real – that's to say, more faithful to the truth throughout. It takes great art, exquisite form, and rigour such as yours to be able to dispense with the ornaments of style. And yet, to the picture you depict, you add poetry with a lavish hand, whether your characters understand it or not. So take things as easy as possible, so that you may live long and produce much.

I've seen a couple of short articles that didn't seem too hostile to your success, but I don't really know what goes on – politics seems to be swallowing up everything else.

FLAUBERT

Your old troubadour is being greatly berated in the press. Look at last Monday's *Constitutionnel* and this morning's *Gaulois* – they don't mince their words. They call me a cretin and a scoundrel.

I have also been flayed in the *Figaro*. I don't care in the least, but it does surprise me that there should be so much hatred and dishonesty. The *Tribune*, the *Pays* and the *Opinion Nationale*, on the other hand, praise me to the skies. As for my friends – they speak to me about everything except the book. Nevertheless, it is selling very well despite the political situation. In short, I have gathered very few laurels so far, and have been wounded with no rose petals.

You can guess what's coming. No one (absolutely no one) is coming to my defence. Therefore if you would care to take on that role you'd oblige me. If it embarrasses you, do nothing.

SAND

The thing is done. The article will go off tomorrow. I'm sending it to…whom? The answer, please, by telegram.

FLAUBERT

La Liberté will print your article immediately. How can I thank you? I long to say all kinds of affectionate things. I have so many in my heart but none comes to my fingertips.

SAND

Come to spend Christmas with us and escape New Year's Day in Paris. It's so tedious! Lina says I'm to tell you, you'll be allowed to wear your dressing gown and slippers all the time.

FLAUBERT

Your article hasn't yet appeared in *La Liberté*. Politics, I think, is the only reason for this delay. I assure you the hostility to your old troubadour is *personal*. That is evident in the articles. Fortunately, I'm not sensitive!

SAND

If you don't come we'll be shattered and you'll be an ungrateful monster. You must stay with us a long, long time: we'll have some more larks on New Year's Eve and Twelfth Night. Ours is a foolish, happy household, and now is a time for recreation.

FLAUBERT

Agreed, dear master! I'll leave for Nohant on Thursday by the nine am train.

Music.

SAND
(*She reads from her diary.*)

Snow and rain all day. We were merry! The little girls were delighted with Flaubert's presents. He enjoyed himself like a schoolboy. Christmas tree on the stage. Presents all around.

We lunched at noon. Then we went out into the garden – even Flaubert, who wanted to see the farm. We went all over the place. Introduced him to Gustave the ram.

The little girls were sweet. At three o'clock Maurice decided to put on an impromptu show. Flaubert was in stitches.

Lolo performed all her dances. Flaubert dressed up as a woman and danced the chachucha. It was grotesque; everyone went wild.

Music fades.

FLAUBERT

I had a good journey back. The worst was the stretch from the Jardin des Plantes to the rue de Clichy. The Paris streets were abominable, and in my cab I was frozen. All the way, I thought only of Nohant. I cannot tell you how touched I was by your welcome. What splendid, lovely people you all are!

SAND

Where are you? Are you in Paris, in the midst of this turmoil? What a lesson it is for countries that want to have absolute masters! France and Prussia cutting one another's throats over matters neither of them understands! So here we are, plunged into great disasters, and it will all end in oceans of tears, even if we win. Round here you see nothing but poor peasants weeping over their children going off to fight. Will this horrible experience teach people at last that war must be abolished or civilization will perish? The position here this evening is that we know we've been defeated. Tomorrow, perhaps, we'll know we've been victorious. And in either case, what good or advantage will come of it? I must admit *my* heart fails me: there's still a *woman* inside the old troubadour, and this human butchery reduces me to tatters. I tremble too for all my children and friends who may get cut to pieces. And yet in the middle of it all my soul revives and even has flashes of faith. We need these harsh lessons in order to realise our own foolishness, and we must make good use of them.

FLAUBERT

I arrived in Paris on Monday and left on Wednesday.
Now I know what the Parisian is really like! For I've
seen such stupidity! Such cowardice! Such ignorance!
Such presumption! My compatriots made me want to
vomit. Perhaps this country *deserves* to be punished, and
I fear it will be. It's impossible for me to read anything
whatever; let alone to write. I spend my time like
everybody else, waiting for news. Ah! If it weren't for
my mother I'd certainly have joined up by now. Not
knowing how to keep busy, I've volunteered as a nurse
in Rouen. My inaction is stifling me: I feel I'm about to
burst. If the Germans besiege Paris, I'll go and fight. My
rifle is ready. But until then I'll remain at Croisset
because I must. I'll tell you why. The vile things I
witnessed in the capital are enough to add years to a
man's life. Ah! How I wish I were dead, not to have to
think about all this! Poor literature!

SAND

We're alive. Nohant is being ravaged by a terrible
smallpox epidemic. We were offered hospitality in the
south of France, but didn't want to leave our own area,
where we might be able to make ourselves useful at any
moment, though we haven't much idea how to set
about it. So we're back here with the friends who live
nearest our own deserted home, and are waiting to see
what happens. The thing is to escape pending disaster.
We mustn't say, or believe, that it's impossible. We
mustn't despair of France: she's expiating her own
folly, but she'll be reborn no matter what. Perhaps we
ourselves will be carried off. What difference does it
make whether we're killed by a bullet or by
pneumonia? We die just the same. Let's die without
cursing our own species!

FLAUBERT

For six weeks we've been expecting those Prussian gentlemen to arrive, from one day to the next. We keep listening, thinking we hear gunfire in the distance. What horrors! It makes one blush to be a man. If we have a victory on the Loire, their coming will be delayed. But will we have that victory? When I feel hope I try to suppress it. And yet deep within me, despite everything, I can't help hoping a little, just a little. I don't think there can be a sadder man than I am in the whole of France. And any attempt to console me irritates me. What breaks my heart is one, human ferocity; two, the conviction that we're about to enter an era of stupidity. And now literature seems to me a vain and useless thing. Shall I ever be capable of writing again? I find it impossible to devote my attention to anything. I spend my days in gloomy, devouring idleness. My niece Caroline is in London. My mother grows older by the hour. Every Monday we go to Rouen and stay there till Thursday, to escape from the solitude of the country. Then we come back again.

Oh! If only I could flee to a country where there aren't any uniforms and one doesn't hear the sound of drums! Where there's no talk of massacres, where one doesn't have to be a *citizen*. But the earth is no longer habitable for us poor Mandarins!

SAND

Let's hope we can soon have a chat and tell one another all about what's happened during our 'separation'. I wouldn't mind anything so long as this hateful war comes to an end!

FLAUBERT

I am choking on gall. These officers who smash your
mirrors with white-gloved hands, who know Sanskrit
and fling themselves on your champagne, who steal
your watch and then send you their visiting-card, this
war for money – these civilized savages horrify me
more than Cannibals. If we take our revenge, it will be
ferocious. And you can be sure we'll be thinking of
nothing but avenging ourselves. Mass murder is going
to be the object of all our efforts! I cherish the dream of
going to live in some peaceful country in the sun.

SAND

Where? What country is going to be peaceful in the
struggle between barbarism and civilization which will
spread all over the world? And isn't the sun itself a
myth? Either it refuses to come out or it scorches you to
a cinder. And so it is with everything on this
unfortunate planet. But let's go on loving it just the
same, and get used to suffering on it.

You don't tell me how you found your delightful nest
in Croisset. The Prussians occupied it; did they knock it
about, dirty it, steal from it? Your books, your bibelots
– were they all still there? Did they respect your name?
And your study? If you can get yourself to work there
again, your mind will be at peace once more.

I'm waiting for mine to get better; I know I have to
forward my own cure by means of some kind of faith,
and though that faith has received many knocks, I've
made it my duty to do so.

Tell me whether the tulip tree suffered from the frost
this winter, and whether the peonies are doing well.

I often make the journey there in my mind, and see your garden and its surroundings again. How much has happened since!

FLAUBERT

No, the Prussians did not loot my house. My study they respected. I had buried a large box full of letters, and hidden my voluminous notes. All that, I found intact. When the railway journeys become possible again, come and see me. Your old troubadour has been waiting a long time. Your letter this morning touched me. What a fine fellow you are, and what a great heart you have!

SAND

I haven't written to you – I've been so completely, profoundly distressed. It will pass, I hope, but I'm ill with the illness of my country and my species. It looks to me as if we're all heading into the unknown. Have you got more spirit than I have? If so, give me some!

FLAUBERT

Why are you so sad? Mankind is displaying nothing new. So I am not disillusioned now. I believe that the crowd, the herd, will always be detestable. Nothing is important save a small group of minds. The idea of equality (which is all that modern democracy is) is an essentially Christian idea and opposed to that of justice. Posterity will consider us very stupid, I'm sure. As for the worthy 'People' – 'free and compulsory' education will be the end of them. When everybody is able to read the *Petit Journal* and the *Figaro*, they won't read anything else. The press is a school for stultification, because it absolves people from thinking. Ah, my dear good master, if you could only hate!

That is what you lack: Hate. Despite your great sphinx eyes, you have seen the world through a golden haze. That comes from the sun in your heart. But so many shadows have loomed that you no longer see things for what they are. Come, now! Shout! Thunder! Take your great lyre and pluck the brazen string. The Monsters will flee.

SAND

It's beyond my powers to believe that progress is only a dream. Without that hope, no one can do anything. There's no point in going on educating the few if it's not in the hope that they'll influence the many. Just let me suffer – it's better than, as Shakespeare says, 'calmly contemplating injustice.' When I've drained my cup of bitterness I'll recover. I'm a woman, I have feelings of affection, pity and anger. I'll never be a sage or scholar.

If a natural society is to survive, its first law must be mutual service, as with the ants and the bees. In animals we call this collaboration Instinct. In man, Instinct is Love, and whoever omits Love omits Truth and Justice.

FLAUBERT

The life I've led this winter has been enough to kill three rhinoceroses. My poor mother has become unsociable, intolerable. What a decline! What a change. She can no longer walk alone. And her frailty is heartrending. How sad it is to watch the slow deterioration of people you love. How sad it is, the indifference that creeps into our hearts! We're looking for a lady companion for her.

SAND

I may know of someone who'd do. Should she be good at reading and conversation?

FLAUBERT

My dear good master, my mother has just died! Je vous embrasse.

SAND

I am with you all the time, day and night, my poor dear friend. I wish I could be there with you. All I can do, my little one, is offer a motherly heart which, though it cannot make up for any loss, suffers closely and keenly with your own, in all your misfortunes. If you feel at all like travelling and lack the wherewithal, I've just earned a few sous, which are at your disposal. Don't stand on ceremony with me, any more than I would do with you.

Music.

FLAUBERT

Today I'm at last beginning to hear the birds singing and see the fresh green of the leaves. I've stopped resenting the sunshine! If only I could feel like working again, I'd be saved. Your letter moved me to tears. How good you are! What a wonderful being!

I have no need of money at the moment, thank you. But, should I feel the need, it is certainly to you I would turn. Shall I have the fortitude to live absolutely alone here, in solitude? I doubt it. I'm growing old. My niece cannot live here now. She already has two places of her own. 'My poor old lady' was very fond of you. It would be sweet to see you here, in her house, *now,* while her presence still lingers.

SAND

Why don't you come to see us here with Mme. Viardot and Turgenev? You like and admire them, you know all of us here adore you, and yet you run away and stay alone. It strikes me you have too strong a tendency to regard happiness as possible, so that the absence of happiness, which is our chronic state, surprises and angers you. You avoid your friends, you bury yourself in work, and time spent on loving or on letting yourself be loved you regard as wasted. Why don't you get married? Being alone is horrible, deadly, and it's cruel to those who love you, too. Isn't there some woman you love, or whom you'd like to love you? Have her to live with you. Or isn't there some young sprig somewhere of whom you might suppose yourself the father? Bring him up, forget yourself in him. Living for oneself is a bad thing, living all the time inside the self. Please, please listen to me! You're keeping an exuberant nature shut up in jail! You're trying to turn a kind and tender heart into a jaundiced misanthropist. In short, I'm worried about you and am perhaps saying stupid things.

FLAUBERT

I do not think of happiness as being possible – but tranquility, yes. That's why I keep away from what irritates me. I am unsociable; therefore I flee Society. The slightest discussion with anyone at all exasperates me, because I find everybody idiotic. All talk is about politics – and *such* talk! Where is there the least sign of an idea? What is there to hold on to?

What cause is there to be passionate about? As for living with a woman, marrying, as you advise, it's a prospect I find fantastic. Why? I have no idea. But that's how it is. Perhaps you can explain. The feminine existence has never fitted in with mine. And then I'm not rich enough. And then, and then… Besides, I'm too old. And also too decent to inflict my person on another in perpetuity. Deep down, there's something of the priest in me that no one suspects.

SAND

You've not right not to be happy! Perhaps it would have been better if the 'feminine feeling' you say you've snapped your fingers at had found a place in your life. I know things 'feminine' are noxious but perhaps to be happy one needs to have been unhappy first. I've been unhappy, and I know all about it. But then I'm so good at forgetting!

FLAUBERT

Don't worry any more about your troubadour. I hope to get over it. I've had a number of sombre periods in the past, and always come out of them. Everything wears itself out, the spleen along with the rest. I expressed myself badly. I didn't say that I scorned 'feminine feeling.' I have loved more than anyone – a presumptuous statement, which means 'like anybody else, and perhaps even more than just anybody.' I have experienced all kinds of affection: 'storms of the heart' have rained down on me and then, Chance, the force of circumstances, has gradually intensified my Solitude, until now I am alone, utterly alone.

SAND

Come and read me your new book and we'll talk about getting it published.

FLAUBERT

Publish? Why – in these abominable times? To earn
money? What a joke! As though the money were an
adequate reward for one's work! And besides, how can
one weigh the Labour? I write not for the reader of
today, but for all readers as long as language exists. So,
why publish? To be understood, applauded? Is there,
now, I don't say admiration or understanding, but any
sign of the slightest attention being paid to works of art?
Where is there a critic who actually reads the book he
judges? Ten years from now perhaps no one will know
how to make a pair of shoes, so frightfully stupid is
everyone becoming! All this is to tell you that until
better times (in whose advent I have no faith) I shall
keep my new book in a cupboard.

SAND

My ambition has never flown as high as yours. You
want to write for *all time;* I think I shall be completely
forgotten, perhaps severely denigrated, in fifty years.
That's the natural fate of things that are not of the
highest order. What I've tried to do is rather act upon
my contemporaries, even if I influence only a few, and
make them share my idea of goodness and poetry. Up
to a point I've attained this goal: at least I've done and
continued to do my best to reach it; and my reward is
to draw always a little nearer. So much for me. For you,
as I can clearly see, the goal is much greater and success
more distant. That only means you ought to be even
calmer and more contented than I am, so as to be more
in harmony with yourself. Your temporary rages are
good. They're the result of a generous temperament,
and as they're neither malicious nor vindictive I like
them! But your sadness, your weeks and weeks of
spleen, I don't understand, and I don't like them at all.

FLAUBERT

Don't take the dramas of my 'rage' too seriously. Don't go thinking I'm counting on Posterity to avenge the 'indifference' of my contemporaries. I meant only this: when you don't address yourself to the Crowd, it's only right that the Crowd shouldn't reward you. That's Economics. Now I maintain that a work of art cannot be evaluated, has no commercial worth, and cannot be adequately compensated. Conclusion: if the artist has no money of his own, he *has* to starve. A charming situation. I am not at all *sure* of writing good things, or that the book I'm at present thinking about will turn out well. That doesn't stop me from undertaking it. I think the idea is original – no more than that. Ah! How I wish I could admire myself.

SAND

Bring me your book. I want to hear it and live it with you. If you can bring Turgenev with you we'll be very glad and you'll have the most delightful travelling companion. Have you read *Fathers and Sons*? Isn't it marvellous?

FLAUBERT

The gigantic Turgenev has just left my flat. It's so difficult to arrange anything with him. I greatly missed you at Mme. Viardot's a fortnight ago. She sang arias from Gluck's *Orpheus*. I can't tell you how beautiful it was – utterly sublime. What an artist that woman is! What an artist! Hearing her sing consoles one for existing.

Music: 'Che puro ciel' from Orfeo ed Euridice by Gluck.

SAND

Talent, will and genius are just as much natural
phenomena as volcanoes, mountains, winds and stars.
Nature alone can speak to the intelligence.

I've been so ill all summer, and am still having such
trouble with my innards, that I don't know if, when the
time comes, I'll be up to travelling next winter. The
hope of seeing you will spur me on, you may be sure.
But I've been very shaky since I entered my seventies. I
did so love stumping about, but now I can't walk any
more without the risk of horrible pains. I work all the
more, and paint watercolours in my leisure hours.
Aurore consoles me. I'd have liked to live long enough
to see her married.

FLAUBERT

Your old troubadour hasn't been very lively for the last
six weeks. Stomach and intestinal pains, nervous
distress, ultra-black mood – that's about the size of it. I
think these may all be mere symptoms of anxiety: the
frightful book I'm beginning weighs on me so heavily
that it's crushing me in advance. In short, I've been in a
pitiable state. Just the last two days things have been
somewhat better. The change of air has revived me.

Otherwise, dead calm. France is sinking slowly, like a
rotten hulk. One has to be here, in Paris, to have an
idea of the universal degradation in which we're
floundering.

The thought of these spasms haunts me: When I'm not
fretting about my work I think only of the dead. And
I'm going to say something very pretentious: nobody
understands me! I belong to another world.

SAND

Poor, dear friend. The sadder you grow, the more I love you. How you fret, how sensitive you are to life! For what you complain about is life. Yet it's never been any better, for anyone, ever. The more we're in advance of our own time the more we suffer. We move like shadows beneath a layer of clouds through which the sun shines fitfully, and we keep appealing to the sun, which is helpless. It's up to us to clear away our own clouds.

You love literature too much. It will kill you, and you won't kill human stupidity. That poor dear stupidity which I don't hate – I look at it through motherly eyes. For it's a kind of infancy, and all infancy is sacred. Yet what hatred you've vowed against it, and how you make war on it! You've got too much knowledge and intelligence. You forget there's something higher than art – wisdom. And art, at its greatest, is nothing but the expression of wisdom. Wisdom comprehends everything: beauty, truth, good –and enthusiasm. It teaches us to see something outside ourselves that is higher than what is within us.

But I shan't be able to change you. I shan't even be able to make you understand how I see and understand happiness; by which I mean the acceptance of life as it is!

There is one person who could change you, though, and save you; and that's old Victor Hugo, for in part he's a great philosopher as well as being the great artist that you need and that I am not. I think he'll be a calming influence. I'm not stormy enough now for you to be able to understand me. But I think he's retained all his thunder, while at the same time acquiring the gentleness and mercy of age.

See him – see him often, and tell him your troubles.
You think too much of the dead. You're too ready to
suppose they're at rest. They are not. They're like us.
They're still exploring.

FLAUBERT

I've put aside my big novel to write a little mediaeval
trifle. It transports me away from the modern world,
and does me good. I'd like to do something terse and
violent. But I still lack the string for the necklace.

SAND

So you're going to get back to the grindstone? So am I,
because I've done nothing but hang around waiting for
my time to be up.

So what shall we be doing? You'll go in for Desolation,
I'll wager, while I go in for Consolation. I can't forget
that my own conquest of despair was due to my will,
and to a new way of seeing things that is completely
opposite to the view I once had. I know you disapprove
of personal attitudes entering into literature. But are
you right? It's not for me to give literary advice, but I
think you lack a more encompassing view of life. Art
isn't merely painting or description… Besides, real
painting is full of the soul that wields the brush. Nor is
art only criticism and satire. I want to see man as he is.
Not good or bad, but good and bad. It seems to me
that your school of writers tends too much to stay on
the surface. By dint of striving after form it underrates
content. It addresses itself to a literary audience. But that
audience doesn't really exist. We are human beings,
before we are anything else.

And we want to find Man at the heart of all stories and
facts. That's what was wrong with *L'Education*

Sentimentale, which I've thought about a lot, wondering why a book so weighty and well written should have aroused so much rancour. The fault lay in the fact that the characters are influenced by facts, but never grapple with them.

FLAUBERT

I don't 'go in for Desolation' wantonly: please believe me! I'm only too full of convictions. I'm constantly bursting with suppressed anger and indignation. But my ideal of Art is that the artist reveal *none* of this, and that he appear in his work no more than God does in Nature. Man is nothing. Work is everything. You say, 'It's not for me to give you literary advice,' but why not? I want your advice. I long to hear your opinions. Who should give advice and express opinions if not you?

SAND

We're buried in snow. I adore this kind of weather: the whiteness is like a universal purification, and indoor amusements are even more cosy and pleasant. How can anyone hate winter in the country? Snow is one of the most beautiful sights in the whole year!

I don't say humanity's on the way to the heights. I happen to think it is, in spite of everything, but I don't argue about it. For my part, I want to tend upwards till my last gasp, not because I either expect or need to find a 'haven' for myself elsewhere, but because my only pleasure is to stay with the people I love on the path that leads upward. Before long you will gradually be entering upon the happiest part of life: old age. It's then that art reveals itself in all its sweetness; in our youth it manifests itself in anguish. You have acquired a degree of learning which I shall never attain. So you are a hundred times richer than any of us – and yet you howl as if you were poor.

FLAUBERT

Ah, thank you from the bottom of my heart, dear master. You have given me an exquisite day: only today have I read your two stories. This morning I immediately took up your volume and devoured it at one sitting. I think it's perfect: two gems! You have never done me anything but good, and I love you tenderly. I've begun another tale called *Histoire d'un Coeur Simple.* You will see from this work (and you will recognise your own direct influence) that I am not as obstinate as you think. I believe you will like the underlying humanity of this little work.

SAND

I'm better, after stomach cramps that were enough to make one go blue in the face, and were horribly persistent too. Physical pain is a salutary lesson so long as it leaves your mind free. You learn to bear and even overcome it. Your have a few bad moments when you just flop on the bed, but I always think of what my old village priest used to say when he had gout: 'Either it will pass or I shall.' And he used to laugh, he was so pleased with his witticism. We're having an extraordinary spring. The ground is strewn with flowers and snow at the same time, and you get frozen fingers picking violets and anemones.

Music.

FLAUBERT

A few days later, Mme. Sand took to her bed. She knew she was dying. Nothing could relieve her. She died after more than a week of intense suffering.

One had to know her as I did, to realise how much femininity there was in that great man, and the vast tenderness of her genius. Her name will live in unique glory as one of the great figures of France.

I began *Un Coeur Simple* exclusively for her, solely to please her. She died when I was in the middle of my work. Thus it is with all of our dreams.

Music fades.

The End.